The Library of Explorers and Exploration

# HERNANDO DE SOTO

## Trailblazer of the American Southeast

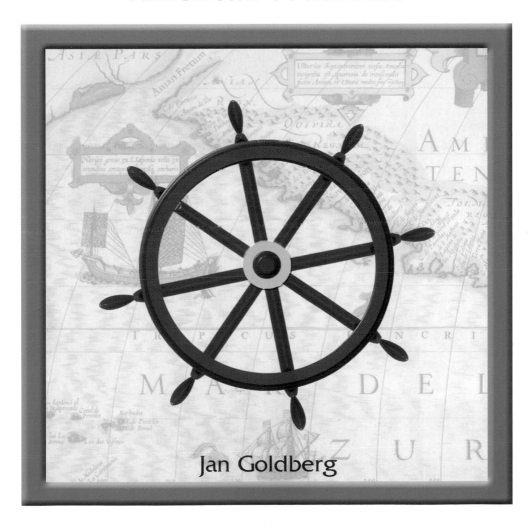

Jan Goldberg

the rosen publishing group's
**rosen central**

*To all the members of my family.*
*Each of you is special and precious. With much love.*

Published in 2003 by The Rosen Publishing Group, Inc.
29 East 21st Street, New York, NY 10010

First Edition

**Library of Congress Cataloging-in-Publication Data**

Goldberg, Jan.
Hernando de Soto : trailblazer of the American Southeast / by Jan Goldberg.
    p. cm. — (The library of explorers and exploration)
Summary: Portrays Hernando de Soto as both a pirate and explorer who, while a failure in some ways, had a lasting influence through such actions as introducing pigs to the Americas.
Includes bibliographical references and index.
ISBN 0-8239-3623-6 (lib. bdg.)
1. Soto, Hernando de, ca. 1500–1542—Juvenile literature.
2. Explorers—America—Biography—Juvenile literature.
3. Explorers—Spain—Biography—Juvenile literature.
4. America—Discovery and exploration—Spanish—Juvenile literature.
5. Southern States—Discovery and exploration—Spanish—Juvenile literature. [1. De Soto, Hernando, ca. 1500–1542. 2. Explorers.
3. America—Discovery and exploration—Spanish.]
I. Title. II. Series.
E125.S7 G65 2002
970.01'6'092—dc21

                                                    2002000334

*Manufactured in the United States of America*

# CONTENTS

# INTRODUCTION

## A PIRATE AND AN EXPLORER

Imagine for a moment that the well-known explorer Hernando de Soto was alive today. He would no doubt be famous for the many thousands of miles he traveled in search of new adventures and riches. He might be considered one of the wealthiest men in the world, and people would undoubtedly be amazed at how he shared his prosperity with others. He would be respected as the commander in chief of thousands of loyal troops. News of his travels and discoveries would be broadcast daily on every radio and television station around the globe and printed on the front page of every newspaper. He would be a regular guest on the talk-show circuit, and his picture would be on the cover of the most important magazines. Children everywhere would admire him, and toy companies would

Hernando de Soto was one of the explorers and conquerors of Peru. He traveled throughout what is now the southeastern United States under constant attack by the native peoples. De Soto died of fever in Louisiana in his early forties.

This painting depicts domestic life in sixteenth-century Europe. Although the subjects in the picture look content, life in those times was hard and punishing. Half of all children born in Renaissance Europe did not live past the age of five. Towns were a maze of narrow, crowded, and filthy streets, and the bubonic plague and periodic droughts and famines took many lives.

manufacture Hernando de Soto action figures. There might even be a movie made about his life, or he could be the star of an action-packed Saturday morning cartoon.

But things were very different in de Soto's time, the sixteenth century. Instead of flying on a private jet from country to country and reaching his destination in mere hours, he sailed in crude ships for weeks and even months at a time. Instead of being driven around each country once he arrived, he had to ride his horse or walk. Instead of being able to call or e-mail his wife or boss (the king of Spain) to report on the progress of his expeditions, he wrote letters that probably took months to get to their intended recipients, if they got there at all. Instead of staying in five-star hotels and dining in fancy restaurants, he camped outside almost every night, even during the bitter cold of winter, and cooked his food—when there was any food to be found—over an open fire. And of course there were no newspapers, radios, televisions, or magazines to report on the importance of his explorations.

Since there were also no computers during de Soto's time, the exact details of his expeditions could not be electronically recorded and instantly printed for everyone to read. The information we have about his life and his journeys comes from the handwritten journal of at least one man who accompanied de Soto on his two voyages, and from historians who have scrutinized and compared those journals and other official documents over the years.

Since there are several different accounts, many of the facts of de Soto's voyages are in dispute. In addition, some information may have been lost in the translation from Spanish to English. Some experts believe that de Soto was cruel and hostile to the Native Americans in the

New World. Others say he was one of the kinder and more compassionate European explorers. Through his search for gold and other riches, he became an explorer in the true sense of the word—finding new adventures, exploring uncharted lands, and meeting new people.

No one knows for sure what kind of man he was, but we are certain that Hernando de Soto journeyed to the New World—Central America, South America, Cuba, and a large section of southeastern North America. Whatever his personality and motives, he certainly earned a place in history.

# 1

# BOYHOOD DREAMS

*Here, boy, touch the gold of the Indies. One day you will follow in the footsteps of the other Extremadura men; for there is ample land to be discovered, and few people live there.*
—A friend of Francisco Méndez de Soto, speaking to Francisco's eight-year-old son, Hernando

As a boy, when Hernando de Soto gazed out the window he saw golden wheat, grazing sheep, and a few people walking down a lonely road that wound southward across the mountains of central Spain. Several years later, at the same window, he noticed that more people were traveling in that direction. Instead of a lone laborer making his way to the fields, there might be a group of young men traveling that road together on foot. Young de Soto wondered where the men were going. Could their destination be the seaport of Cadiz, 300 miles away? He knew that Christopher Columbus had sailed from Cadiz on his later voyages to the New World. While peering out the window, he became infatuated with the idea of traveling to distant lands to find adventure.

This is a picture of a town in Hernando de Soto's home region, Extremadura, Spain. A harsh and empty province in de Soto's time, it is now called the Cradle of the Conquistadors. The explorers Hernán Cortés, Vasco Núñez de Balboa, and Francisco Pizarro and his brothers also came from there. In fact, one in six of all Spaniards who sailed to the Indies in the sixteenth century came from Extremadura, including nearly half of de Soto's 600 or so men.

Playing among the ruins of an ancient castle or fortress, de Soto and his friends liked to spend their time on grown-up games. Whether on horseback or on foot, the games frequently included dueling with wooden swords and lances. De Soto often pretended that he was the hero from his favorite book, *The Virtuous Knight Amadis of Gaul*. In the story, the knight is deeply in love with a princess but is unable to win her hand in marriage until he proves how courageous he is.

De Soto was from a family of six, which included his mother, Leonor Arias Truoco, and his father, Francisco Méndez, two younger sisters, Catalina and Maria; and his older brother, Juan. As the eldest son, Juan would inherit their parent's estate.

Most historians agree that de Soto was born in 1500. However, it actually could have been as early as 1496. With record keeping the way it was hundreds of years ago, we don't know for sure. In fact, we don't know much about de Soto's childhood that can be authenticated. Most experts agree that he grew up in a manor house in Jerez de los Caballeros, a town of about 8,000 people located seventy-five miles northwest of Seville, Spain. The region is known as Extremadura. We know that de Soto was strong and taller than average. In fact, it is said that at fourteen years old he looked more like nineteen and was considered stronger than most grown men.

This is a portrait of King Ferdinand II investing a vassal (a feudal lord). Under the feudal system of the time, all land belonged to the king, who granted it to vassals. In return, vassals swore loyalty to the king, paid him a portion of the lands' income, and maintained a standing army for him. Pedrarias Dávila, de Soto's patron, was reputed to be one of Ferdinand's favorite feudal lords and military commanders.

Rumored to be his mother's favorite, de Soto tried to please her by taking subjects like grammar, rhetoric, history, and logic in school. His mother hoped he would grow up to be a priest or scholar. His father wanted to locate a patron, someone who would support him financially, so that de Soto would be able to continue his education in Salamanca. But none of this was to be. De Soto preferred to spend his time in other ways. He enjoyed wandering to the nearby river, playing at the ruins of an ancient castle, or spending his time in the stables with horses. Given de Soto's later reputation as an expert horseman and fighter, he obviously devoted much time as a boy to mastering these skills.

## Planning His Future

Though both of de Soto's parents were of noble blood, they were short of money. Consequently, de Soto was forced to figure out a way to support himself. It was considered improper for noblemen to do manual labor, so he had to find another way to make a living. Luckily, a Franciscan friar named Diego, who was the local director of studies, didn't feel very confident about de Soto's schoolwork and agreed to provide him with a letter of introduction to a nobleman called Pedro Arias de Avila, who was planning an expedition. Also known as Pedrarias Dávila, he was considered one of King Ferdinand's favorite military leaders.

This woodcut depicts Vasco Núñez de Balboa claiming the Pacific Ocean for the king of Spain in 1513. Balboa was from the same town as de Soto and the two are believed to have been neighbors. Historians speculate that Balboa may have sparked the fire of exploration in de Soto.

In 1514, while still only a teen, de Soto was sent by his father to the port city of Seville. With tears in their eyes, his mother and sisters saw him off. Since traveling on foot was considered undignified, de Soto traveled on his most valuable possession: his horse, Lucerno. Arriving on a March morning, he and Lucerno galloped through the gate of Macarena and moved on to see Dávila. The meeting was very successful, and de Soto immediately became a page in Dávila's household.

De Soto longed for more than his parents could ever have dreamed of experiencing or owning. His inspiration to find gold and glory may have come from a neighbor named Vasco Núñez de Balboa. When de Soto was about thirteen years old, Balboa led an exploring party from Darién, a small Spanish colony in the New World, across the Isthmus of Panama. Balboa discovered a great body of water that he named the South Sea. Today it is known as the Pacific Ocean.

There is an old legend that may or may not be true. As the story goes, when de Soto was about nine years old, a neighbor approached him one day showing him flakes of gold. Supposedly he said, "Hernando, if you don't have this, you don't have anything." Whether this fable is true or not, the sentiment behind it burned inside de Soto throughout his entire life.

# 2

# SEEKING NEW HORIZONS

*We agree with you that there is only one God; this we have always believed. But that the pope rules the universe and can give away our lands to your king . . . Giving away lands that are not his—let him come and take them!*

—Chieftain of the region of Cenú

At the point in southern Spain, where the Guadalquivir River meets the Atlantic Ocean, an expedition led by Colonel Pedrarias Dávila set sail from Sanlúcar in early April 1514. Onboard the flagship were Dávila's wife, Doña Isabel de Bobadilla, and two of her young daughters, Isabel and Elvira. Dávila had also brought along three teenage boys to serve as his pages. One of these young men was Hernando de Soto, who was just fourteen years old.

This hand-colored woodcut depicts Pedrarias Dávila attacking natives on the island off the Isthmus of Panama. Dávila took the fourteen-year-old de Soto on this trip. To young de Soto, war and conquest were glorious occupations: He had the chance for adventure and the opportunity to restore the family fortune.

Things did not go well at first. A raging storm at sea forced the whole fleet of ships to return to Sanlúcar, and many seasick members of the expedition changed their minds and went home. On a second try, the expedition set sail again on April 11, 1514, and reached Gomera, in the Canary Islands, at the end of the month. While there, de Soto and the rest of the crew were told to inspect the ships thoroughly and prepare them for the long voyage across the ocean. They gathered food, such as dried fish and meat, and cheese, as well as fresh water. They also brought other supplies, like horses, and seeds to plant. On May 9, 1514, they continued on their journey westward.

During his time aboard the ship, de Soto learned a lot about life at sea. When he wasn't busy with his own chores, he memorized the names of all the parts of the ship and found it very interesting to watch the sailors do their work. He became friends with a fellow assistant named Diego San Martín, and also with the ship's navigator, Juan Vespucci, a great-nephew of the Italian explorer Amerigo Vespucci, for whom North America and South America are named.

De Soto's favorite pastime, however, was to stroll the ship's decks with Doña Isabel and her two daughters. Doña Isabel reminded de Soto of his own mother, and during their walks she taught him about good manners, chivalry, poise, and taste in clothing. More important, it was during this time that de Soto fell in love with Doña Isabel's daughter, Isabel, who was then just nine years old. Knowing that Isabel was in love with de Soto, too, and not knowing how Dávila would feel about a "lowly" servant in love with his noble daughter, Doña Isabel decided to keep the relationship a secret from her husband.

# De Soto's First Exploration

On June 3, 1514, the fleet arrived at the group of islands known as the Lesser Antilles and anchored off the coast of the island of Dominica. De Soto and his friend San Martín were part of a small party sent ashore by Dávila to explore the island, get grass for the many horses they had brought with them, and find fresh water for the crews. San Martín disappeared while the group was on the island, and de Soto and several other men searched for him long into the night. San Martín came back to the ship at one o'clock in the morning, cheerfully telling his fellow crew members of his many adventures while walking around the island. But Dávila was so angry that San Martín had wandered off alone and caused so much trouble that he had him killed on the spot. De Soto was very sad about losing his friend and lost much of his excitement about the trip. He finally realized that the long voyage might not only be filled with great riches, but also with death and destruction.

This navigational map of America was created by Gerardus Mercator in 1595. Mercator, a German cartographer also known as Gerhard Kramer, is the father of modern world maps and globes, and his maps are still used today. Due to the impossibility of accurately projecting a sphere on a flat surface, Mercator's maps are not completely accurate. While his maps proved to be great navigational tools because of their accurate representations of shapes, they do not show the continents and hemispheres in proper proportion. Instead, the southern continents appear much smaller than they actually are.

This painting depicts the battle of Pavia in Lombardy, Italy, between the armies of Francis I of France and the Holy Roman Emperor Charles V. The guns the combatants carry are harquebuses and muskets. Harquebus refers to any of several small-caliber long guns operated by matchlock or wheel-lock mechanisms. Harquebuses were popular in the 1400s and were widely used. This battle may have been the first in which hand firearms carried the day.

At ten o'clock in the morning on June 12, 1514, the fleet dropped anchor off the coast of what is today the country of Colombia. They saw warriors on the shore, wearing feather headdresses and carrying bows and arrows. A party of sixty men went ashore with orders from Dávila not to attack unless they were attacked first. The sailors were able to scare away the natives with two shots from a harquebus, a large and heavy type of gun. The next day, Dávila sent another party ashore, and this time de Soto was invited to go along. This group found three deserted villages from which they took blankets, clothing, fishing nets, a few pieces of gold, a large sapphire, and some emeralds.

The fleet then continued on toward the city of Santa María del Darién, where Dávila was to be governor. The Spanish explorer Vasco Núñez de Balboa had founded the town, which was located in what is now the country of Panama. In September 1513, just about a year earlier, Balboa had also "discovered" the Pacific Ocean (then called the South Sea or the Southern Ocean) on the southern side of the Isthmus of Panama. Balboa then settled in Panama with the princess Anayansi, the daughter of a powerful Indian chieftain, and he was there to greet Dávila's fleet when it arrived.

Balboa learned that he and young de Soto were from the same region in Spain. The two became friends, and Balboa offered to give de Soto fencing lessons. De Soto soon became one of the best riders and lancers in Dávila's army, and he entered tournaments to show off his skills.

During his time in Central America, Balboa had made friends with the natives, and everything was peaceful. Dávila, however, was very different from Balboa. He was jealous of all that Balboa had accomplished, and he wanted to get rid of him. He didn't want to be friends with the natives; he believed that they should be

This picture is from a series of sixteenth-century books of European adventures in the Americas. It shows a meeting with a native ruler, Panchiaco, who seeing Balboa's thirst for gold, offers to show him where to find more. The volumes and illustrations were produced by Theodor de Bry, a Frankfurt goldsmith, engraver, printseller, and bookseller. Most of the pictures were made from first-hand observations and are among the earliest authentic images of the New World.

used only for finding gold. He often sent his men to establish new towns and torture the natives in order to get them to tell the Spaniards where the gold was hidden. Even though Balboa had established peace throughout the land, the natives were soon learning the ways of war instead.

One day, Dávila sent Balboa on a very dangerous mission, hoping that Balboa would be killed. However, Balboa completed the mission successfully and returned to

Darién with even greater honor and more popularity than before. This made Dávila even angrier, so he invented a charge of treason against Balboa and had him thrown in prison, under the threat of death. De Soto often visited his friend in prison, but he didn't want Dávila to find out.

Even though the governor could be very cruel and de Soto probably didn't agree with a lot of the things he did, de Soto still felt he should be loyal to Dávila. After Dávila had Balboa killed a short time later, de Soto secretly helped Anayansi give him a proper Christian burial on a hillside nearby. Anayansi then told de Soto she was returning to her people, for they were much less savage than the Spaniards.

After Balboa's death, de Soto remained a guard for Dávila. He was made a captain after going on several successful expeditions around Central America. In June 1520, de Soto returned from a trip to what is now Costa Rica to learn that his beloved Isabel had gone back to Spain with her mother and sister.

A week later, he received a secret message from her: In a book she had written the words, "I will wait for you all my life, darling." Hernando was growing anxious to return to Spain, but he knew he must first find his fortune in the New World so that he could give Isabel the luxurious life she deserved.

# Nicaragua

Around 1525, Dávila sent de Soto with Captain Fernández de Cordóba to conquer the area now known as Nicaragua. During the long mission, de Soto discovered that de Cordóba intended to capture Nicaragua in his own name, not in Dávila's name. De Cordóba asked for de Soto's help, but de Soto refused out of loyalty to Dávila. Though Dávila was a very cruel man, he was the father of the woman de Soto loved, and de Soto had spent many years at his side and learned a lot from him.

When de Cordóba learned that de Soto was on Dávila's side, he had de Soto put in prison. But thirty of de Soto's fellow soldiers, who also disagreed with de Cordóba, overcame the guards and freed de Soto. Twelve of them accompanied him on the long journey back to Panama to warn Dávila of what de Cordóba was up to. They then went with Dávila back to Nicaragua, where de Cordóba was immediately imprisoned and then killed by Dávila's men.

Dávila rewarded de Soto well for his loyalty, but de Soto felt that he still did not have enough

This illustration is taken from one of Theodor de Bry's volumes on European adventures in the New World. It shows how the Spaniards on Hispaniola (modern-day Haiti and Dominican Republic), having worked the natives to death, began to import slaves from Guinea to work in the gold mines.

wealth to be able to return to Spain a rich man. He faithfully remained at the governor's side until Dávila's death at the age of ninety-one, on March 6, 1531.

After Dávila died, de Soto remained in Nicaragua with two of his friends, Hernan Ponce and Francisco Compañón. The three men decided that there must be a better way to find gold than to try and steal it from the natives, so they formed their own mining company. The business was very profitable, and de Soto seemed content for a while. But after his friend Compañón died of a sudden illness, de Soto decided he had had enough of the New World and wanted to go back to Spain. About this time, however, he overheard some men talking about a fellow Spaniard named Francisco Pizarro, who was planning an expedition to conquer the great Inca kingdom in Peru.

# 3

# THE INCAS
# AND BEYOND

*You may return to Panama and live in poverty, or follow me to Peru and become rich. Let the true Castillians choose what they would rather be.*

—Francisco Pizarro

The Incas called their empire the "four corners of the world." It was as large as the present-day states of Texas, Arizona, New Mexico, and California combined, and it covered what are now Peru, Ecuador, and parts of Colombia and Bolivia. Over six million people were part of the civilization. They were very advanced in agriculture and engineering. They built fine roads, including a twisting, mountainous highway that stretched 1,000 miles from the northern capital of the kingdom, Quito (now the capital of Ecuador), to the southern capital, Cuzco (in present-day Peru). Most important, it was believed that the Incas had great wealth and more gold and other treasures than they knew what to do with.

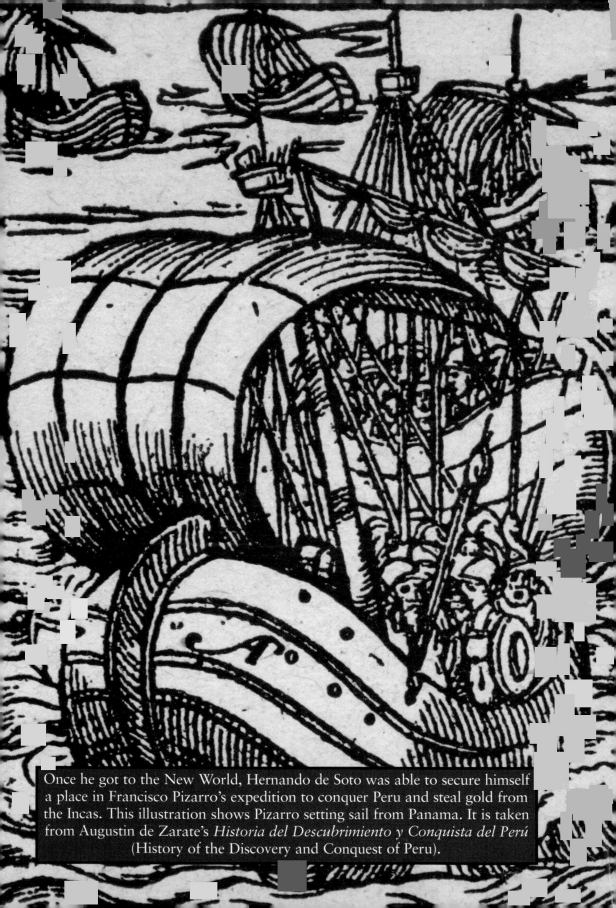

Once he got to the New World, Hernando de Soto was able to secure himself a place in Francisco Pizarro's expedition to conquer Peru and steal gold from the Incas. This illustration shows Pizarro setting sail from Panama. It is taken from Augustin de Zarate's *Historia del Descubrimiento y Conquista del Perú* (History of the Discovery and Conquest of Peru).

De Soto didn't want to miss out on a chance to add to his riches, so he sold his property in Nicaragua, bought two boats, and headed back to Panama with 100 loyal Spanish soldiers. He had been promised the title of lieutenant general in Pizarro's army, but when he arrived in Panama, he learned that Pizarro had given the title to his own brother, Hernando Pizarro. De Soto was disappointed and considered returning to Spain instead, but Pizarro assured him that he could still be second in command, even though his brother had the title. The lure of gold was very strong, too, so de Soto was convinced to stay. He and the other soldiers joined Pizarro's men, and a crew of over 200 set out for Tumbez, in the northwest corner of what is now Peru.

## Atahuallpa

After founding the city of San Miguel de Piura about ninety miles south of Tumbes, Pizarro decided to lead an expedition to Cajamarca, high in the Andes Mountains, where the Inca king Atahuallpa was camped. He sent de Soto and twelve other men ahead as scouts, and on the way they met one of Atahuallpa's men. They nicknamed this man Long Ears, because the huge gold earrings he wore had pulled his earlobes out of shape. He was also adorned with several gold wristbands, ankle bands, and necklaces,

This hand-colored woodcut is a portrait of Atahuallpa, the last Inca king of Peru. Hernando de Soto was the first European to ever meet him. Although the Spanish ambushed and killed thousands of his men, some say Atahuallpa formed a bond with his captor, de Soto.

and was wearing a beautiful, brightly colored woven coat. The men were astonished and could not stop themselves from staring excitedly at Long Ears's attire. If a lowly messenger was wearing so many pieces of gold and other wonderful things, what must his king be like? Surely the Incas must be as rich as the men had heard—or perhaps even richer!

The Spaniards led Long Ears to Pizarro's camp, where Long Ears arranged for Pizarro to meet with Atahuallpa in Cajamarca. De Soto's job was to prepare the men and the horses for the difficult journey over the steep Andes Mountains. They arrived in Cajamarca on November 15, 1532, and found the city nearly deserted. After making camp in the empty buildings of the city, Pizarro sent de Soto and fifteen other men to Atahuallpa's camp, about three miles away. De Soto found Atahuallpa in his large mansion and became the first European to see the mighty king. In turn, de Soto was also the first European that Atahuallpa had ever seen.

De Soto graciously delivered Pizarro's message: "Greetings, My Lord. I bring you the salutation of my governor, Don Francisco Pizarro, who earnestly wishes to pay his respects to you in person, in the name of our lord, the king of Spain." Atahuallpa agreed to meet them in Cajamarca the next day but de Soto knew that Pizarro was planning to take the Inca king prisoner. He told Pizarro that if they were going to capture Atahuallpa, they should make sure he was not harmed.

Atahuallpa came to Cajamarca the next day, as promised, with thousands of spear-carrying warriors (though some say they were only ceremonial weapons), hundreds of servants, and several hundred of his noblemen. They carried the king on a couchlike pedestal, called a litter, and he was wearing a large and heavy gold crown. The Spaniards were hiding in buildings, and when Atahuallpa and his men reached the city square, Pizarro's men attacked them. After a thirty-minute battle, 2,000 Incas were dead in the square and several hundred, including Atahuallpa, had been taken prisoner by the Spaniards.

While Pizarro's men were holding Atahuallpa captive, de Soto was assigned the duty of watching over him. In the months that followed, it is said that the two men grew to like one another. De Soto taught the great king how to play chess, how to say a few words in Spanish, and how to read a few words. In return, Atahuallpa taught de Soto some words in his own language.

One day, Atahuallpa realized that Pizarro and his men only wanted one thing from the Incas: gold. He offered Pizarro a whole room full of gold in exchange for letting him go. Even though Pizarro couldn't believe that Atahuallpa had enough gold to fill the large room he was kept in, he agreed to the plan. Over the next two months, Atahuallpa's men brought load after load of valuable gold to the room in wheelbarrows. There were

This sixteenth-century engraving by Theodor de Bry shows Hernando de Soto asking Atahuallpa to meet with Francisco Pizarro in Cajamarca. Atahuallpa and thousands of his warriors met Pizarro the next day, where the Spaniards ambushed the Incas and captured their king.

shiny gold plates, cups, pots, statues, fountains, and urns, and there were also many silver pieces, which were placed in another room nearby.

When the room was finally full of gold, just as Atahuallpa had promised, the fortune was worth what would be about $1.5 billion today. Pizarro divided it up, giving small portions to his foot soldiers and slightly larger portions to his senior officers (including de Soto). Since it was customary to set aside a fifth of the loot for the Crown, he kept the rest for himself.

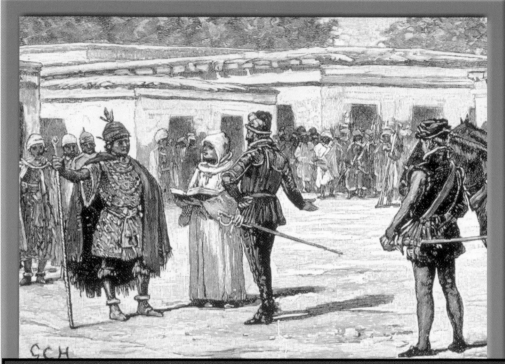

This hand-colored woodcut depicts the meeting between Francisco Pizarro and the last Inca king, Atahuallpa, on November 16, 1532. Invited into the city of Cajamarca, Atahuallpa was ambushed and taken prisoner. The Inca gave a room full of gold as ransom but the king was executed anyway.

But Pizarro still did not release Atahuallpa. De Soto questioned Pizarro about why he would not set the king free after Atahuallpa had kept his promise. He suggested that Pizarro send Atahuallpa to Spain, where the king could decide his fate. Pizarro said he'd think about it, but then he sent de Soto on a scouting trip to the distant region of Guamachuco. De Soto was supposed to find out if Atahuallpa's people were planning to attack Pizarro's camp in order set their king free, but de Soto quickly found that there was no such plan.

When he returned to Cajamarca, de Soto found out that he was too late; Pizarro's men had killed Atahuallpa two days earlier. De Soto was so angry with Pizarro that he told him he wanted to go back to Spain. He had enough gold now to marry Isabel, and he was looking forward to returning home to her. But Pizarro gave de Soto even more gold and convinced him to stay just a little while longer, to help him conquer the city of Cuzco, the southern capital of the Inca Empire. De Soto agreed to stay, and by the year 1535 he had become governor of Cuzco and had added to his growing fortunes, which would be worth about $4.5 million today.

De Soto finally returned victorious to Spain in 1536 and married Isabel, who had waited for him for sixteen years. De Soto and Isabel lived in an elegant mansion in Seville and enjoyed throwing big parties, and de Soto never got tired of talking about the rugged mountains of Peru or the steamy jungles of Panama. The king of Spain, Charles V, awarded de Soto many honors.

# The Search for More Riches

De Soto could have lived a noble, wealthy life with Isabel in Spain, but by 1537 he was getting restless. He longed for more adventures, and he wanted to march through places where no Europeans had ever been. He had heard

stories of a place in the New World called La Florida. It had been "discovered" in 1513 by a Spaniard named Juan Ponce de León, who had been searching for slaves as well as the fountain of youth. Legend said that the fountain of youth was a magical spring with waters that had the power to make old men young again.

Ponce de León found the peninsula of what is now Florida, which he thought was an island, in late March. The expedition landed near present-day Saint Augustine, and Ponce de León claimed the land in the name of Spain, calling it Pascua Florida. After exploring the land up and down the coast, he returned to Puerto Rico and lived there until 1521, when he led a second expedition to Florida. This time Ponce de León took with him 200 men, hundreds of farm animals, and farming tools. They landed on the western coast, possibly in Charlotte Harbor, just north of where Fort Myers is today. As soon as they came ashore, however, Native Americans attacked the party and Ponce de León was severely wounded by a sharp arrow. The group quickly sailed to Cuba, where Ponce de León died of his injury shortly after they arrived.

Juan Ponce de León, shown here, was the first European to "discover" Florida. He landed near modern-day Saint Augustine and claimed it for Spain. He thought it was an island and named it La Florida in honor of Easter Sunday, the day he first spotted its coast. Easter Sunday is known as Pascua de Flores in Spanish.

After hearing about Ponce de León's adventures, de Soto was convinced that he would find twice as much gold in Florida than he had found in Peru. King Charles V asked de Soto to conquer Florida in his name, and he gave de Soto the title of governor of Cuba so he could make Cuba his headquarters. He also asked de Soto to pay for the trip with his own money, the fortunes he had brought back from Peru. Isabel didn't want to be away from her husband, so she decided to travel with him.

De Soto began assembling young men, boats, horses, and supplies for the voyage. Thousands of people who had heard about the riches of the New World volunteered to go along, but de Soto chose only the youngest and strongest men, about 600 of them. He made sure that his new army included not just soldiers, but also surgeons, blacksmiths, carpenters, and priests. By the spring of 1538, the expedition was ready.

# 4

# THE EXPLORATION OF FLORIDA

*This duty weighs upon me more than every other, and for the attentions you will bestow, as befits your goodness, I shall be under great obligations.*
—Hernando de Soto, in a July 1539 letter to the justice and board of magistrates in Santiago de Cuba

Hernando de Soto's expedition to conquer Florida began on April 7, 1538, when his ships set sail from Sanlúcar. There were ten vessels in de Soto's fleet, including two very large ships, a galleon, a caravel, and also two small brigantines. The 800-ton flagship that carried de Soto and Isabel was called the *San Cristóbal*. Twenty other ships bound for Mexico accompanied them on their voyage across the ocean, so there were thirty magnificent vessels in all. On the launch day, trumpets blared, ceremonial gunfire exploded, and people cheered and waved as the ships left the port.

The fleet first stopped in Gomera, in the Canary Islands, to stock up on food and other supplies. Gomera was the same place de Soto had stopped with Dávila on his earlier voyage. Each vessel's commander had the duty of making sure that he had all the supplies he was responsible for. Some gathered tools, such as saws, axes, shovels, and hammers, while others stocked up on weapons, like falconets, powder kegs, swords, and lances. Some stored farming equipment on their boats, like hoes, shovels, spades, and seeds, and others were responsible for wine, oil, vinegar, fruit, and cooking utensils.

After forty-two more days of sailing, the expedition reached Cuba. They stayed for a year while de Soto assumed his role as governor and gathered 400 more men and supplies for his voyage to Florida. He sent a small group ahead to Florida to find a good place to land and unload their supplies, and they returned with news of a large harbor on the western shore. Toward the middle of May 1539, de Soto's fleet set sail from Cuba with 1,000 men, hundreds of horses and pigs, vicious war dogs, and all the supplies their vessels could carry. Isabel stayed in Cuba to tend to the government, but de Soto told his wife that he would return for her in a year or two with twice as much gold as he had before.

Fifteenth-century Spanish galleons were among the best battleships of the time. They were large enough to function as either fighting ships or merchant ships. Spain also used them on expeditions and to defend the loot they won. It took more than 2,000 trees to make some of the larger galleons. Their average weight was 400 tons, the same as two jumbo jets, and they traveled at four to eight knots, or about five to nine miles per hour.

On about May 30, 1539, after nineteen days of cold and rough sailing, the group reached the harbor that de Soto's scouts had found earlier. They called it the Bay of the Holy Spirit, which is where Tampa Bay is today. The men began unloading their cargo and were almost finished when a large group of Native Americans attacked with tomahawks (war axes), arrows, and knives.

The battle ceased when a white man on horseback rode out of the woods waving his arms and yelling something in Spanish. He was a fellow Spaniard named Juan Ortiz, and had been stranded there for eleven years. Ortiz had been part of the unsuccessful expedition to Florida led by Pánfilo de Narváez in 1527, but he was captured by one of the tribes and forced into slavery.

The cruel chieftain of the tribe, Hirrihigua, tortured Ortiz for a year and a half, leaving Ortiz with burns and scars all over his body. Hirrihigua wanted to eventually kill Ortiz, but his wife and daughters pleaded with him to let Ortiz live. Then, without Hirrihigua knowing it, they helped Ortiz escape to a nearby tribe whose chieftain, Mucoco, was much less cruel. Mucoco let Ortiz remain with his tribe and protected him from Hirrihigua for more than nine years.

After hearing Ortiz's story, de Soto gave him clothes to wear and asked him to come with them on their journey and serve as interpreter, so that they would be able to

This woodcut shows early explorers coming ashore on the Florida coast. The tribes along the Florida coast were known for the ferocity with which they defended their lands. In fact, Ponce de León died from a wound inflicted in a battle with one of these tribes.

communicate with the Native Americans they met along the way. Ortiz went to tell Mucoco of his plans and soon returned with Mucoco himself.

The chieftain said he came to warn de Soto and his men. He told de Soto that traveling further inland would be very dangerous, because of the unfriendly natives and the slimy swamps that were infested with alligators and insects. He said that he would give de Soto and his men all the land they would ever need if they would stay and settle near his tribe instead.

FLORIDAE AMERICAE PROVINCIAE
Recens & exactissima descriptio
Auctore Iacobo le Moyne cui co-
gnomen de Morgues, Qui Laudo-
nierum, Altera Gallorum in eam
Prouinciam Nauigatione comitat?
est, Atque adhibitis aliquot militibus,
Ob pericula, Regionis illius interi-
ora & Maritima diligentissime
Lustrauit, & Exactissime dimensus
est, Obseruata etiam singulorum
Fluminum inter se distantia, ut ipse-
met redux Carolo.ix Galliarum
Regi, demonstrauit.

This sixteenth-century map of Florida and Cuba was drawn by Theodor de Bry for a series about great voyages of the time. The map is inaccurate; Cuba is too large, and the long peninsula of Florida is stunted.

De Soto asked Ortiz to tell Mucoco that he was grateful for the chief's kind offer, but that they had come there to explore the land, not to settle on it. He also gave Mucoco many fine gifts that he had brought with him from Spain.

Around this time, de Soto also uncovered an amazing secret among his soldiers: One of them was a woman! Her name was Francisca Hinestrosa, and she came on the voyage disguised as a man because she didn't want to be away from her husband, one of de Soto's soldiers.

Everyone thought that de Soto would be furious, because he had given strict orders that no women were to come with them from Cuba. Apparently, though, de Soto was quite amused, because he allowed her to remain with them and work as a cook and nurse.

On June 15, 1539, de Soto left 100 men at the Bay of the Holy Spirit to guard the supplies while he and 900 of his men began marching inland. As they were trying to make their way through the first muddy swamp they encountered, a group of natives attacked them.

The Spaniards lost a lot of horses, but the men were protected from the natives' arrows by the murky water. This made de Soto realize that they would need more protection from the natives' weapons, so he sent a group of men back to the bay to fetch their heavy cotton jackets, which were three inches thick.

This woodcut depicts de Soto's expedition setting up camp in Florida. In 1537, Holy Roman Emperor Charles V, who was also king of Spain, named de Soto governor of Cuba and Florida. But unless de Soto could colonize Florida, still a largely unknown land, it was a meaningless title.

Soon the group reached a territory belonging to a chieftain named Acuera. With Ortiz's help, de Soto offered the tribe friendship, but Acuera refused. He had heard about Spaniards who robbed the tribes, destroyed their homes, murdered them, and left. He told de Soto and his men to go away. Many other tribes must have heard about the Spaniards, too, because de Soto's group found several deserted villages along the way; the natives had probably fled when they heard the white men coming. Explorers often stole from local villages. De Soto and his men stole vegetables, raisins, prunes, and acorns they found in the villages because they were so hungry. Though they were running out of their own food, de Soto wouldn't let them kill any of the pigs they had brought along for emergency food.

The soldiers kept marching through Florida. Sometimes they met friendly tribes of Native Americans, and sometimes unfriendly tribes attacked them. Their heavy coats protected them from the arrows when they were attacked, and they usually managed to make their way without losing too many of their own men.

## Battling Native Americans

Soon the mighty army crossed the Ocala River and found itself in north central Florida, where the city of Gainesville is today. This area was ruled by a chief named Vitachuco, who had vowed to defeat the Spaniards. With the help of his tribe's medicine men, he had tried to cast evil spells on de Soto and his troops. When his black magic didn't work, however, he agreed to meet with de Soto and pretended to be friendly, saying that he and his tribe would willingly escort the Spaniards through the unfamiliar territory. He also invited de Soto and his men to watch a parade of thousands of his warriors in a nearby field.

Though de Soto was suspicious of Vitachuco, he and his men went with the chief to the field, where they found warriors wearing war paint lined up in battle formation. Vitachuco raised his hatchet and all of the warriors shouted a war cry. De Soto also gave a signal to his own men and someone quickly brought him his horse so that he could lead his men into battle with his lance held high.

Even though they were outnumbered, the Spaniards had horses and much better weapons than the native warriors. The warriors' arrows and tomahawks could not cut through the heavy cotton jackets of the Europeans, and several thousand of Vitachuco's men retreated into the forest. About a thousand others ran into a small lake, swimming and fighting all night long while the battle continued. By dawn, only fifty warriors had surrendered, and de Soto told

his men to capture the others and bring them to the water's edge, where he gave them food and let them rest. Seven warriors, however, still refused to leave the water. De Soto asked them why they would rather die than surrender to him and they told him that they had promised their chief that they would defeat the Spaniards.

Vitachuco, the chief, was among the more than 900 warriors de Soto's men had taken as prisoners, and he was still determined to win. He secretly ordered each of his men to kill one Spaniard apiece when he gave the signal.

One day, de Soto invited Vitachuco to sit with him for a meal, and it was then that Vitachuco signaled his men. Vitachuco reached over and attacked de Soto, but a Spanish soldier quickly killed him. The other warriors continued fighting, and since they no longer had any weapons of their own, they used whatever they could find in the camp—things like burning logs, stones, sticks, heavy jugs, and pots of boiling water.

After all the warriors had been killed by the Spanish, the soldiers marched to the west. By November 1539 they had reached the town of

This image shows a scene from de Soto's expedition in Florida in which a Spaniard drags captive natives. De Soto made enemies of the indigenous people by seizing their grain, burning their villages, and enslaving their people. He also used specially trained war dogs to attack the natives during battles. The cost was high to both sides, however, as many of de Soto's soldiers were killed in battles and ambushes.

Apalachee, which is now the city of Tallahassee, Florida. De Soto sent some of his bravest officers and soldiers back to the Bay of the Holy Spirit to tell the ships to sail north to the coast of Apalachee Bay, just south of Apalachee. The rest of them stayed in Apalachee for the winter. When the ships arrived in Apalachee Bay, de Soto told them to sail westward and find another harbor for the following winter. They returned and reported that they had found Achusi about 150 miles away. (Achusi is now called Pensacola.) De Soto then told the ships' captains to sail back to Cuba and get more crossbows, muskets, shoes, clothing, and other supplies. He also gave them messages and gifts to present to his wife Isabel, and instructed them to meet back in Achusi the following October.

# 5

# NEW EXPEDITIONS

*White Chief, may the Sun shine upon you and defend you. Your magic powers are well known to us and we seek your friendship. At first, we committed the error of thinking of resisting you, but only foolish men persist in their errors. Wise and rational men know when to change their mind. We are here to wish the Palefaces a happy stay and help them, whatever they may need.*
—Chief Guachoya, April 1542

On March 3, 1540, when the long, cold winter had ended, de Soto and his troops began marching again. Though they were all tired, hungry, and frustrated in their search for gold, they began heading northeast. Eventually they crossed into what is now the state of Georgia. They reached Cofitachequi, near what is now Savannah, Georgia, in the beginning of May. They had heard that Cofitachequi was ruled by a young, pretty, powerful, and very wealthy woman. The princess, whose name was Cofita, was very friendly and welcomed the Spaniards into her village. Some say her people offered de Soto and

his men food and lodging, and that she gave de Soto a strand of large pearls from around her neck. Others say de Soto tricked and robbed her. When she found out that de Soto was looking for gold she said she had plenty, and sent some of her people to get it for him. But when they returned, they had no gold—only iron and copper—and indicated that they didn't know where to find any gold. Cofita gave de Soto more pearls and a number of soft, warm deerskins.

De Soto and his men continued northward into present-day South Carolina, North Carolina, and Tennessee. Everywhere they went, the Native Americans welcomed them because Princess Cofita had sent messages to the tribes telling them of the friendly Spaniards. From the natives, the Spaniards learned how to eat lizard and wild turkey, how to grind corn for flour, and how to make tortillas. One soldier came back from a scouting trip and reported that he had seen "a large, unusual cow, with very big hooves and a humped back." This was probably the first time a European had seen the great American bison, or buffalo.

This woodcut depicts de Soto meeting Cofita, the leader of the Cofitachequi in 1540. According to some accounts, she told de Soto that her people had little food and had been afflicted by a terrible plague (possibly due to the diseases, such as smallpox, that were brought to the New World by European expeditions). The Cofitachequi took de Soto to their temple, which had a roof of cane mats and was decorated inside and out with shells and pearls.

Hernando de Soto and his men are shown journeying across America on one of their expeditions in this painting by Frederic Remington.

# Tuscaloosa

It was almost October 1540, time to head south again and meet the ships in Achusi. From Tennessee, de Soto's troops entered present-day Alabama and marched until they reached the land ruled by the great chief Tuscaloosa. They were at the Alabama River, probably just southwest of what is now the city of Montgomery. The chief had heard about the Spaniards and had acted friendly to them, but he was being deceptive just as Vitachuco had been. Tuscaloosa wanted to defeat them, not be friends with them. De Soto invited him to go with them to the next village, and he gave him a horse to ride. Tuscaloosa had never even seen such an animal before, and he was so tall that his feet almost touched the ground when he got on the horse.

Everything seemed fine when they all rode into the village. But as soon as de Soto and his men got off their horses, Tuscaloosa gave a signal and thousands of warriors from several different tribes came running out of the buildings to attack the Spaniards. De Soto was very worried, because most of his men were still on a mission in a nearby village. He and his soldiers fought the natives for hours, and during the fight de Soto was hurt.

When the battle was over, it is reported that more than 2,500 Native Americans had died. Sixty Spaniards had perished, and 250 others were seriously injured.

De Soto followed the Savannah River to the Blue Ridge Mountains, eventually reaching Malvilla (modern-day Mobile, Alabama). There he defeated a Native American tribe but suffered heavy losses himself. This engraving shows a Native American village built within palisades, such as would have been found in Malvilla.

Almost all of the Spaniards' supplies and food had been destroyed in a fire. They spent several days cleaning up and helping the people who were hurt. There was only one surgeon left among the ranks, and his medical supplies had all been lost as well.

During this time, de Soto was saddened to find out that many of his men were planning on abandoning him when they reached the ships in Achusi. The men were desperate to end a journey that had brought hardship, danger, hunger, and death—but absolutely no gold.

61

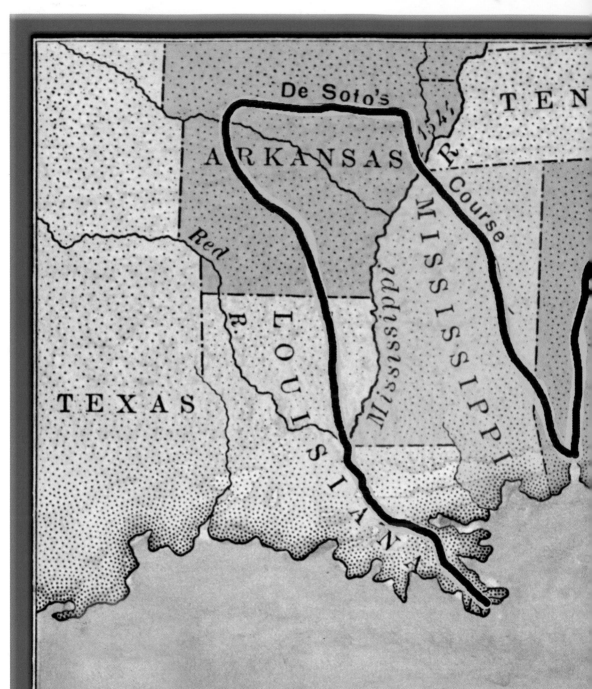

This map shows the approximate route of de Soto's expedition in the New World. For four years, de Soto and his men explored some 350,000 square miles in what is now the southeastern United States. In May 1541, they became the first Europeans to see the Mississippi River.

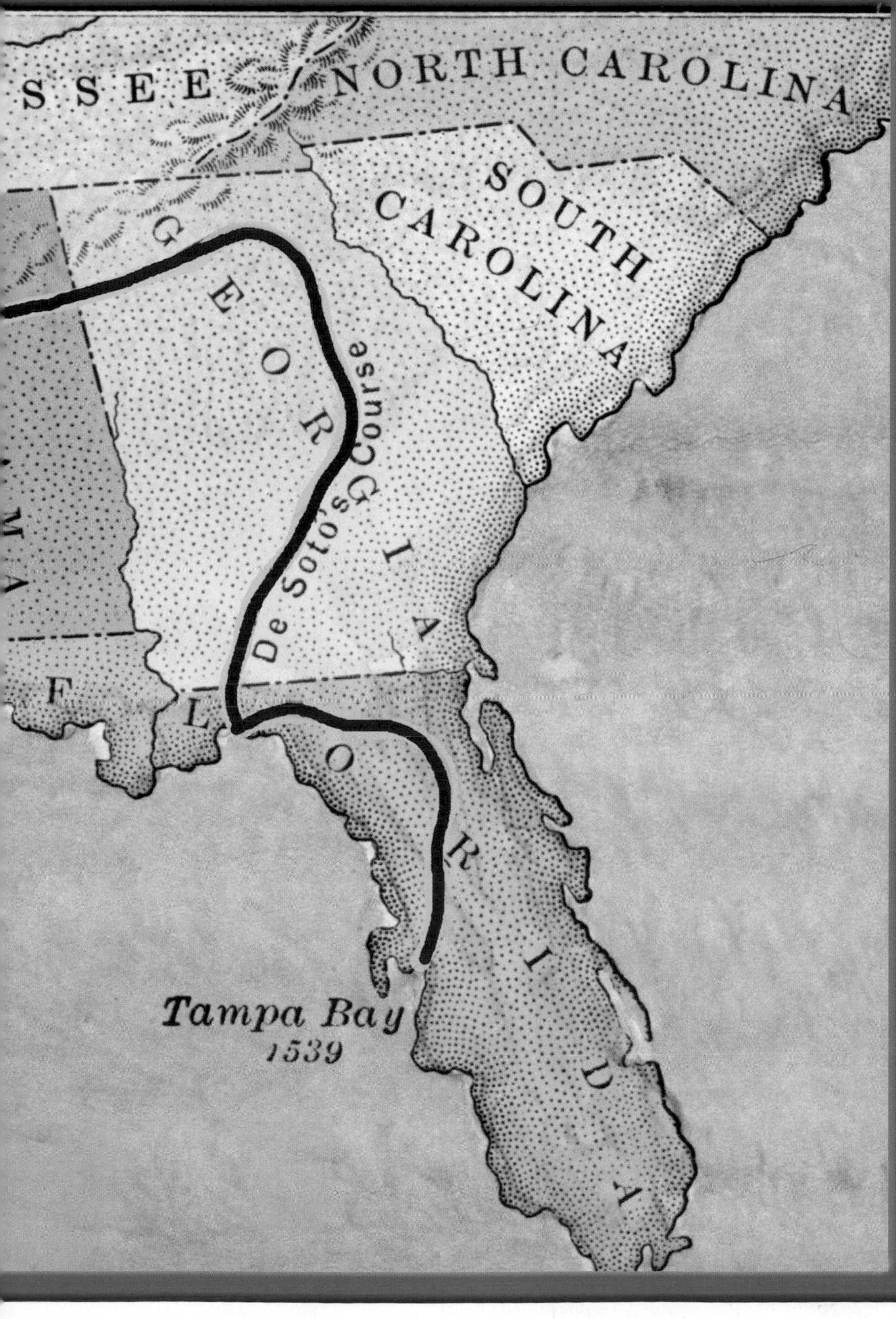
SSEE
NORTH CAROLINA
SOUTH CAROLINA
GEORGIA
De Soto's Course
FLORIDA
Tampa Bay
1539

# The Mississippi River

After hearing about the plan, de Soto decided to go north instead of south so that he wouldn't be left alone with just a few loyal soldiers. His troops started marching again on November 18, 1540. By mid December, they had found an abandoned village named Chicaza near the place where the Yazoo and Tallahatchie Rivers meet in central Mississippi. Because there were plenty of empty houses for the soldiers, de Soto decided they would stay there for the winter.

When spring came, they started marching northwest. But one day in early May 1540, in an area just south of what is now Memphis, Tennessee, de Soto gave the signal for everyone to stop. Up ahead, he had just seen an enormous river, larger than any he had ever seen before. It was the majestic Mississippi River, and they were the first Europeans to see it. Still, de Soto was not happy. He wanted to return to Cuba a hero, and he believed that the Pacific Ocean and large amounts of gold could be found on the other side of the river.

De Soto decided that he had to take his men across the river, but it was so wide that he knew they would never be able to cross it without first building boats. So, they spent twenty days making rafts and barges big enough for everyone and finally crossed the great river on June 18, 1541. It had now been two years since de Soto said good-bye to his beloved Isabel in Cuba.

De Soto confers with Native Americans on the banks of the Mississippi River. De Soto crossed into Arkansas and explored the Ozark Mountains before he fell ill.

After everyone had safely crossed into what is now the state of Arkansas, de Soto ordered his men to take all the rafts apart and save the nails and wood to use later. Then he led them north, following the path of the river, until they found a large village. The friendly chief of the tribe that lived there told de Soto that if the white man's religion was really as powerful as they said it was, then their god would bring much-needed rain to the tribe's very dry crops. De Soto had his men build a tall wooden cross on a hill overlooking the village. They held a religious ceremony around the cross. Three days later, it rained and soaked all of the tribe's crops. From that day on, the Native Americans, encouraged by de Soto, believed that de Soto had magic powers and that he must therefore be immortal, like a god.

For the next ten months, de Soto led his men through territory that would one day be the states of Oklahoma, Louisiana, and Texas. They spent the winter in southeastern Arkansas, and before spring came, de Soto noticed that his men had become extremely thin and dejected.

Sadly, de Soto's trusted adviser and interpreter, Juan Ortiz, died of starvation along with many others. De Soto had started his expedition with over 1,000 men, but now his troops had dwindled to 500. Some had died in battles with the natives, while others had died of hunger or sickness.

When spring came and the men began marching east again, de Soto noticed that one of his men, Diego de Guzmán, was missing. A search party looked for Guzmán for several days, then they heard from some natives that he was living with the nearby Naguatex tribe. Guzmán had married the daughter of the tribe's chieftain and then sent a message to de Soto saying he had found a beautiful woman, all the food he could eat, and many riches, and had no wish to continue the expedition. De Soto didn't want to force Guzmán to leave with his troops since it had been a long and hard journey of more than 2,000 miles. Guzmán stayed with the tribe and became the first European settler in what is now the United States.

By the beginning of May 1542, de Soto was finally ready to give up his search for gold, and all he could think of was returning to Cuba and Isabel. He led his men back to the banks of the Mississippi River, where they began making boats in order to sail down the river and into the Gulf of Mexico.

But on May 14, 1542, de Soto became very sick with a high fever, possibly from malaria. Knowing that he was probably going to die, he called his trusted soldier, Luis de Moscoso, to him and turned over command of the troops. He told Moscoso that he wanted him to continue making the boats so the men could get back to Cuba.

When de Soto died in 1542, his men had to keep his death a secret. Since he had convinced the Native Americans that he was a god, and therefore immortal, if news of his death leaked, they were sure to revolt. So instead of burying him in a grave, de Soto's men lowered his body into the Mississippi River.

In what is now southeast Arkansas, near the river he had reached a year earlier, Hernando de Soto died on May 21, 1542, at age forty-two. Since the Native Americans thought de Soto was immortal, it would be very risky for them to find out about his death, for they would surely attack the remaining soldiers. So, in the middle of the night, the men secretly placed de Soto's wrapped-up body in a hollowed-out log and sunk it in the deepest part of the river where it would not be found.

Moscoso wished to carry out de Soto's orders and finish building the boats, but many of the men had decided they should march west and continue looking for gold. For the next year, they wandered through Arkansas, Louisiana, and parts of eastern Texas, until they finally returned to the river to begin their voyage back to Cuba. They had lost many more men in battles and from sickness and hunger, and by then there were only 311 Spaniards left. After a long and difficult trip down the river and into the Gulf of Mexico, they finally reached Havana, Cuba, in December of 1543.

When de Soto didn't return for Isabel as he had promised, she suspected that her husband was no longer alive. Still, she was extremely distraught when she heard the actual news of her husband's death. Sadly, she was unable to survive without him and died just a short time later.

# 6

# THE EFFECTS OF DE SOTO'S TRAVELS

*If* [Hernando de Soto] *had lived two years longer, he would have repaired the damage done in the past, with the help of the reinforcements he would have requested and received, via the Mighty River, as he had planned. This could have been the start of an empire that today could have competed with New Spain and Peru.*

—Garcilaso de la Vega, 1599

Hernando de Soto didn't discover great riches on his second voyage to the New World. He didn't colonize any areas for Spain or establish any permanent settlements. In fact, when he died on the banks of the Mississippi River, he no doubt thought that he and his mission had been great failures.

To the contrary, history has proven that de Soto and his expedition could indeed have boasted of many great achievements. The more than 300 survivors who eventually made it back to Spain had some written accounts of the journey that described with enthusiasm the beauty of the land, the fertile soil for farming, and the ample supply of fish, game, and other

This woodcut shows Spaniards descending on the Mississippi River after de Soto's death in 1542. Luis de Moscoso took over the expedition and decided to continue with de Soto's plan to build ships and sail down the Mississippi River toward the Gulf of Mexico.

food sources. All of this prompted Spain to send even more explorers to the New World in order to attempt to claim the land for the Spanish and establish colonies in their name.

Several more expeditions headed to Florida over the next twenty years, but all failed. However, the French succeeded in establishing a colony and fort of their own on the Saint Johns River in northeast Florida in 1564. King Philip II of Spain (son of King Charles V) wasn't about to let France have what he wanted, so he finally sent his most experienced and trusted admiral, Don Pedro Menendez de Aviles, to the New World.

De Aviles arrived on the eastern coast of Florida, just south of present-day Jacksonville, on August 28, 1565, and took over the Native American village of Seloy. He named it Saint Augustine and then, with his mighty army and a little help from a devastating hurricane, drove the French out of the Saint Johns area. Claiming the coast of Florida in Spain's name, he began building Saint Augustine while his priests established a number of religious missions for the Native Americans.

Because Saint Augustine was founded forty-two years before the English landed at Jamestown, Virginia, and fifty-five years before the Pilgrims landed at Plymouth Rock, Massachusetts, it is considered the oldest permanent European settlement in North America.

# The River

Of course, being the first European to find the Mississippi River was de Soto's biggest accomplishment. Though he was awed by the size of the river, he did not know at the time how important a discovery it was and how crucial the waterway would one day be to the continent.

When Moscoso and the other surviving Spaniards followed the waterway all the way to the Gulf of Mexico, they found that the river led right through the heart of North America. When this river first leaves its headwaters, Lake Itasca in north Minnesota, it's only a tiny stream, ten feet wide and two feet deep. (It reaches its widest point, nearly three miles across, near Clinton, Iowa.) Yet the entire Mississippi system, which is comprised of the river, its tributaries (like the Missouri River and the Arkansas River), and their branches (including the Platte River and the Wabash River), adds up to over 12,000 miles of navigable waters. These waterways lead to many important cities, like St. Louis, Missouri; New Orleans, Louisiana; Minneapolis, Minnesota; Kansas City, Kansas; Pittsburgh, Pennsylvania, and Cincinnati, Ohio.

This eighteenth-century map of what is now the southeastern United States was engraved by Guillaume Delisle in 1719. The map shows the routes taken by Hernando de Soto in 1540 and by Henri de Tonti in 1702. De Soto was the first European to lead an expedition in this vast region. The area was settled by the French in the early eighteenth century and now comprises several southern states.

After steamboats were invented in the early 1800s, the Mississippi River was the easiest way to transport freight from one place to another. When the country began expanding to the west, however, and out of the reach of the Mississippi system, transcontinental railroads took over as the main way to transport goods. Today, trucks and airplanes are also used for this purpose, of course, but barges and tugboats are still used on the lower Mississippi as an inexpensive way to move large shipments. In fact, the port of New Orleans, just north of where the Mississippi River flows into the Gulf of Mexico, is the largest port in the United States, with freighters and tankers from all over the world docking there every day.

Just as de Soto probably did not realize the importance of his discovery of the Mississippi River, he could not have known other ways in which he influenced the New World, positively and negatively.

# Peaches

The vessels leaving Spain in 1538 carried huge stores of supplies, including ready-to-eat food and seeds to plant to grow more food. The Spaniards had no way of knowing what type of food the New World would provide, or if there would be enough for everyone, so they had to ensure they had everything they needed to survive. They no doubt brought along many types of preserved fruit, and possibly seeds or seedlings as well.

The Spanish introduced fruits like the peach to North America. California, Georgia, and North Carolina are the largest peach producers in the United States.

One fruit they stocked up on was peaches. Though peaches are native to China, they were brought from Persia (now Iran) along silk trading routes. From there, the Greeks and Romans spread peaches throughout Europe as early as 300 BC. Though the Portuguese are credited with bringing them to South America, peaches ended up in North America as a result of de Soto's expedition. The Spaniards shared them with the Native Americans and probably planted the seeds or seedlings as well, and the Native American tribes in turn spread them throughout North America, including southern Canada.

Today, peaches are grown in two-thirds of the United States and rank as the second largest commercial fruit crop in the country, after apples. They are grown mainly in California, North Carolina, Colorado, and the southern states. In Georgia, where de Soto and his men stayed with Princess Cofita and her tribe for perhaps several weeks, peaches are a state icon.

# Pigs and Pork Barbecue

When de Soto chose to include a small group of live pigs as part of his food supply, he couldn't possibly have known the importance those animals would one day have in North American society. Pigs and hogs are members of the swine family, and there are none native to the Americas. They are native to Europe, Asia, and Africa. From pigs, we get food such as ham, bacon, and pork, and other products such as leather for footballs and gloves, and bristles for brushes. The Spaniards brought only a small number of pigs with them, perhaps as few as thirteen. By the end of the expedition that number had grown to more than 700, not including those the group had eaten, the ones that escaped, and those given to the Native Americans.

The Native Americans had of course never tasted the meat, and they became very fond of it. Some sources even say that the natives' desire for pork was the cause of some of the battles between the tribes and de Soto's soldiers. The Spaniards learned an important new method of cooking from the natives: They observed them slow-cooking their pork, turkey, and venison on a wooden or metal framework that was placed over hot coals. It is believed that the Native American word for this framework was *barbacoa*, which is probably the origin of the word "barbecue."

In the years that followed de Soto's expedition, other explorers and settlers brought even more pigs to the New World. Today, the United States is one of the world's leading pork-producing countries.

## Diseases

Although many positive things came from de Soto bringing pigs on his journey, one of the negative consequences of his expedition involved these animals as well. Though they could not have realized it at the time, the Europeans brought several diseases with them to the New World, including swine flu, smallpox, and measles. Eating contaminated meat carried the disease to people, who then spread the germs further through interactions with other humans. Native Americans did not have the same immunities or resistance to such diseases as the Europeans had, and their contact with the newcomers often wiped out

This 1565 illustration by Jacques le Moyne shows methods used by Semiole Indians to treat the sick. European explorers exposed Native Americans to new diseases which killed hundreds of thousands of them.

entire tribes. Natives infected with disease could, in turn, infect members of other tribes. Many of the deadly germs could also live for quite some time on things that the Spaniards touched, such as trade goods.

If you add the number of natives killed by disease to the number who were killed in battles with the Spaniards, it's possible that tens of thousands of native peoples died as a result of the expedition. Some sources estimate that Native American populations in the South may have dropped by more than 90 percent over the 200 years following contact with the Spaniards.

# Christianity

All Spanish expeditions to the New World, including de Soto's, were required by the king to try and establish Christianity as the official religion. The king gave a document called the *Requerimiento*, or "command," to the expedition priests that they were supposed to read to the natives immediately upon contact with them. The priests were not supposed to make war with the natives unless they were attacked, and even then they were supposed to read the *Requerimiento* at least three times before striking back.

The *Requerimiento* was a very bulky document carried in a big leather folder. It informed the natives of the New World that if they would accept that their lands now belonged to Spain, and if they accepted Christianity as their religion, they would not be disturbed. If they didn't accept the terms of the document, however, their possessions would be taken and they would be captured and used as slaves. The document also attempted to explain the basis of the religion.

One important factor made the king's orders nearly impossible to carry out, however: The Native Americans did not understand Spanish. Even with the help of Juan Ortiz, the translator, the natives found it very difficult to understand what it all meant. Those natives who did finally make some sense of the

*Requerimiento* agreed that there was only one god but they could not agree that the king had the authority to take control of lands that were not his. De Soto apparently realized early on in the expedition that reading the document was useless, and some sources say that he ordered his men to stop using it altogether for the rest of the expedition.

Even though the *Requerimiento* was not used by de Soto's priests, the religion of the Spaniards was important throughout the expedition. When the fierce battle with Tuscaloosa's tribes resulted in a fire that destroyed the Spaniards' supplies, the bread and wine that they used for Holy Communion were lost as well. Not being able to perform their religious rituals apparently caused great mental anguish among the troops.

When a tribe asked de Soto to use the power of his religion to bring rain to their dry crops, rain came three days after the Spanish priests erected a cross and held religious ceremonies around it. This led the tribe to think that de Soto had magic powers and was immortal like a God, and there is no way to know what future impact this had on that tribe and neighboring tribes who were told the story.

This engraving made in 1624 by Theodor de Bry illustrates the massacre of Christian priests by Indians, probably in Brazil. The Spanish often used violence to forcibly convert the natives to Christianity, and this led to great resentment among the native people, who had their own beliefs.

Although there is no actual evidence that de Soto converted any of the Native Americans he encountered to Christianity, his expedition in general paved the way for future Spanish expeditions, which in turn established religious missions and eventually helped secure a place for Christianity in the New World.

Unfortunately, de Soto did not accomplish any of the main goals of his expedition. He never knew the importance of finding the Mississippi River; he may have even viewed the wide river as a nuisance and an obstacle because he couldn't cross it without first wasting valuable time building boats. He did not even live to see any of the results of his long years of hard work and determination. He did, however, leave lasting impressions on the history of North America, both positive and negative, that will never be forgotten.

# 7

# DE SOTO'S LEGACY

---

*Understand further that while I live no one shall leave this country, but that we must conquer and settle it, or all die in the attempt.*

—Hernando de Soto

Since the beginning of time, it has been the custom to name people, places, and things after important figures in history. For instance, in the United States, there are at least fifteen cities and towns named for the first president of the United States, George Washington. There are also counties in thirty-one states that are named Washington, plus the state of Washington itself, Washington D.C., and numerous streets, rivers, schools, and much more throughout the country.

Explorers who leave their mark on the territory they roamed, settled, or conquered often have places and things named after them, too. Hernando de Soto's friend, Vasco Núñez de Balboa, who settled in Panama and made friends with the natives after

"discovering" the Pacific Ocean, lends his name to Panama's unit of currency, the balboa. In 1904, the year that work was started on the famous Panama Canal, the government of Panama even introduced a special silver dollar that featured Balboa's portrait. And Amerigo Vespucci, the Italian explorer, had two whole continents named in his honor.

While de Soto doesn't have a continent named after him, his legacy still lives on in our country in many important ways. One product that bears his name was once very well-known in many parts of the world; in 1929, the Chrysler Corporation unveiled a brand-new make of automobile called the DeSoto. The first DeSotos were very advanced for their time, and the company claimed that they were "as daring as their namesake" and "the most exciting car in the world today." Over 80,000 of these cars were sold in the first year of production, and that incredible sales record stood for thirty years.

Though it would be nearly impossible to list each and every place that has borrowed de Soto's name, the following sections offer a state-by-state tour of many of his memorial namesakes, following the path of de Soto's own famous journey.

Many towns, counties, roads, avenues, and monuments in several southeastern states have been named for Hernando de Soto. This picture is of lanterns hanging from a fountain on De Soto Avenue in Coral Gables, Florida.

# Florida

Fort De Soto occupies a tiny island near the entrance to Tampa Bay, around where de Soto's expedition was thought to have landed in May of 1539. During the Civil War, Union troops used the island (later called Mullet Key) and another one nearby to block the Confederates from entering the bay. From high atop the Egmont Key Lighthouse, the Union troops could see whether any Confederates were coming. The actual fort was constructed in 1898 during the Spanish-American War, but it was never the site of a major battle.

Named Fort De Soto in 1900, it is now a beautiful county park, with beaches, hiking trails, fishing, and more, and it was added to the National Register of Historic Places in 1977.

Nearby, in Bradenton, Florida, stands the De Soto National Monument. The facility is operated by the National Park Service, which says that the site "commemorates the landing and legacy of the 1539 expedition of Hernando de Soto." Exhibits in the park's visitor center include artifacts from de Soto's time, including weapons, arrows, and pieces of Native American pottery, plus detailed maps tracing the expedition's route. Visitors can also watch a film entitled *Hernando de Soto in America*. Back outside, hiking along the park's

Visitors walk toward cannons at Fort De Soto Park, in Mullet Key, Florida. The fort was built in 1898 to defend the entrance to Tampa Bay. Fort De Soto has the only four twelve-inch seacoast rifled mortars in the United States.

trail system allows visitors to experience first-hand the coastal swamp environment that the Spaniards had to deal with after they landed. During certain parts of the year, park rangers and volunteers dress in costumes similar to what was worn in the sixteenth century and present programs and demonstrations related to the site. Bradenton is also the location of the Hernando de Soto Historical Society, whose mission is to "keep alive the memory of Hernando de Soto and his landing in 1539 in what is now Manatee County."

Southeast of Bradenton lies DeSoto County, while Hernando County can be found about thirty miles north of Tampa. Continuing north and then to the west, much like de Soto and his group did, the trail leads to the city of Tallahassee, the capital of Florida. In de Soto's time, Tallahassee was the site of the Native American village of Anhaica, and it is where the Spaniards spent their first winter (1539–1540) in the New World.

In fact, the exact spot where they camped is believed to be less than a mile away from the current Florida State Capitol Building. Since the Spaniards were devout Christians, historians also believe that they celebrated Christmas Mass here. If so, it was the very first such celebration in what would one day become the United States. The Spaniards also built some dwellings here that are thought to be the first European-made structures in the United States.

In 1987, archaeologists uncovered the first evidence proving that de Soto and his men did indeed visit the site, so the state of Florida purchased the five acres of land in 1988 in order to protect it from development. Now called the Hernando de Soto State Archaeological Site, it is open to the public. Each January, a reenactment of the Spaniards' winter encampment, complete with appropriate costumes, takes place at the site.

Many natural attractions throughout the southeastern United States are named in honor of de Soto. This beautiful waterfall on Lookout Mountain, Alabama, is called the DeSoto Falls. Another set of waterfalls in Georgia bears his surname, and there is a De Soto National Park in Minnesota.

## Georgia

Though de Soto and his troops didn't spend much time in Georgia, his legacy lives on in the state in a few ways. The small town of De Soto, in Sumter County, is located near the city of Americus in the southwest part of the state.

Across nearly the entire northern tenth of Georgia, just south of the Tennessee border, is the Chattahoochee National Forest. It is believed that the Spanish troops camped somewhere along here on their way to Alabama, after exploring parts of what were to become South Carolina, North Carolina, and the southeast corner of Tennessee. The mountainous national forest is home to several popular hiking trails, one of which is a two-mile trek that leads hikers past two beautiful waterfalls. It's called the Desoto Falls Trail, and nearby is the Desoto Falls Recreation Area, featuring campsites and picnic tables for visitors to enjoy.

## Alabama

Alabama was de Soto's next stop. In the northeast corner of the state is Fort Payne. Here, DeSoto State Park covers more than 3,000 acres along Little River and offers a wide variety of both summer and winter activities, including camping, climbing, kayaking, and snowshoeing. The park's main attraction is the 100-foot DeSoto Falls atop Lookout Mountain.

Southwest of Fort Payne, near the city of Birmingham in the center of Alabama, is DeSoto Caverns Park in Childersburg. Historically, Childersburg was known as Coosa, one of the homes of the great chieftain Tuscaloosa and his tribe. It is believed that Tuscaloosa's battle with de Soto and his army destroyed Tuscaloosa's empire. Though de Soto did not discover the cave, it is thought that he passed right near there.

# Mississippi

Marching west from Alabama, de Soto and his men entered Mississippi. In the southeast corner of the state, stretching almost all the way from the city of Laurel to the Gulf of Mexico, is DeSoto National Forest. At over 500,000 acres, it is Mississippi's largest national forest, and offers horseback riding, hiking, fishing, canoeing, wildlife viewing, and many other nature activities.

In the northwest corner of Mississippi, just south of the Tennessee border, is DeSoto County. The western edge of this county is where historians believe de Soto first saw the Mississippi River on May 9, 1541. Though de Soto's exact route through here is unknown, the Hernando de Soto Memorial Trail goes through the county in an attempt to recreate the Spaniard's route to the river. It also winds near three Native American villages that the explorers supposedly visited before crossing the river in June.

## Tennessee

Since de Soto's discovery of the Mississippi River is thought to have occurred just south of the present-day city of Memphis near the Tennessee-Mississippi border, Memphis honors de Soto and his achievements in a big way: The Hernando de Soto Bridge connects Memphis to Arkansas. In the shape of a large "M," the bridge is the "largest freestanding letter of the alphabet in the world," according to *The Guinness Book of World Records.*

## Arkansas

West of Memphis, in the northeast corner of Arkansas, is the Parkin Archaeological State Park. Scholars believe it is the site of the Native American village of Casqui, visited by de Soto in the summer of 1541, just after he crossed the Mississippi River. An Arkansas Archaeological Survey Research Station was established at the site, and visitors can watch archaeologists working to carefully uncover prehistoric and Native American artifacts. There is also a museum with some exhibits related to Spanish exploration.

This engraving of Hernando de Soto by J. Maca is housed in the Library of Congress in Washington D.C. De Soto is remembered both as a brave and cruel warrior, one who gave up a possible life of wealth to become the first European to chart what is now the southeastern United States.

**HERHANDO DE SOTO:**

*Estremeño: uno de los descubridores y conquis-*
*tador. del Perú: recorrió toda la Florida y venció á*
*sus naturales invencibles hasta entónces: murió*
*en su expedic.ⁿ el año de 1543. á los 42. de su edad.*

## Louisiana

Historical sources can't agree on whether de Soto died in what is now Arkansas or Louisiana. However, a state historical marker in Ferriday, Louisiana, on the banks of the Mississippi River just west of Natchez, Mississippi, reads "Intrepid Spanish conquistador who traversed half of North America, died here at the Indian Village of Guahoya, May 21, 1542. He was buried in the Mississippi River, which he discovered."

# The Last Word About de Soto

Was Hernando de Soto primarily a ruthless conquistador who focused only on his own selfish goals of building a personal fortune in gold? Or was he an ambitious, courageous, fearless, explorer who was kinder than other adventurers of his time? Perhaps more important than his motivation for travel is the evidence of his accomplishments. There is no doubt that his life and travels had far-reaching effects that even de Soto himself could hardly have dreamed of.

# CHRONOLOGY

**1492**  Christopher Columbus reaches the West Indies.

**1500**  Hernando de Soto is born in Jerez de los Caballeros, in the Extremadura region of western Spain.

**1502**  Christopher Columbus reaches Nicaragua.

**1507**  The first world map showing "America" is made by Martin Waldseemüller.

**1513**  Vasco Núñez de Balboa reaches the Pacific Ocean. Juan Ponce de León reaches Florida.

**1514**  In April, de Soto leaves Spain for the New World, part of an expedition led by Colonel Pedrarias Dávila.

**1520**  Dávila's daughter Isabel, whom de Soto is in love with, goes back to Spain but vows to wait for de Soto.

**1527** Juan Ortiz, as part of an expedition to Florida led by Pánfilo de Narváez, is captured by a native tribe and stranded in the New World.

**1531** Dávila dies at the age of ninety-one. De Soto goes to Panama to join an expedition to conquer Peru, led by Francisco Pizarro.

**1532** With de Soto's help, Pizarro's army conquers the city of Cajamarca in Peru and takes the Inca king Atahuallpa prisoner. Pizarro later has the king killed and takes more than $1.5 billion worth of gold from the Incas.

**1535** De Soto helps Pizarro conquer the city of Cuzco, the southern capital of the Inca empire and becomes governor.

**1536** De Soto returns to Spain and marries Isabel.

**1538** On April 7, de Soto, Isabel, and 600 others leave Spain for the New World. They spend a year in Cuba, while de Soto serves as governor and gathers more men and supplies for the next leg of the expedition.

**1539** On May 30, de Soto and his men land in present-day Tampa Bay on the western coast of Florida.

**1541** In early May, de Soto reaches the Mississippi River. His men build boats and the expedition crosses the river on June 18.

**1542** De Soto dies on the banks of the Mississippi on May 21, and his men bury his body in the river.

# GLOSSARY

**brigantine**   A sailing ship with two square-rigged masts.

**caravel**   A small, light sailing ship. In the sixteenth century, caravels had four masts and triangular sails.

**chieftain**   A leader of a group, especially a clan or tribe.

**chivalry**   The qualities of an ideal knight such as bravery, courtesy, honor, and politeness toward women.

**colonize**   To form or establish a colony in a foreign land under the legal authority of the country that the colonists originally came from.

**diligent**   Hardworking, using extra care and effort.

**falconet**   A small cannon used during the fifteenth century and later.

**flagship**  The main ship (commonly the largest) of a fleet of ships, which carried the fleet commander and flew the commander's flag.

**friar**  A monk, or a male member of a religious order.

**galleon**  A large, three-masted merchant ship, used especially by Spain from the fifteenth to seventeenth centuries either for transporting goods or as a warship.

**harquebus**  A very heavy but portable gun from the sixteenth century that had to be lit with a match and was usually fired from some kind of support, like a cannon.

**headwaters**  Small streams that are the sources of a larger river or rivers; the place where a river begins.

**isthmus**  A narrow strip of land that connects two larger land masses.

**onyx**  A type of semiprecious stone with alternating colored layers, often carved to make jewelry and figurines.

**page**  A boy who serves as a messenger and assistant in a royal court and trains to be a knight.

**patron**   One who financially sponsors or supports a
person, an institution, or a cause.

**rhetoric**   The study of efficient or persuasive language,
or the art or study of speaking with elegance.

**smallpox**   A highly contagious and often fatal disease.
By 1980, worldwide vaccination programs had
destroyed the disease.

**treason**   To betray one's own country by waging war
against it or willingly aiding an enemy of that country.

**tributary**   A stream or river that flows into a larger
body of water or the branch of a river.

# FOR MORE
# INFORMATION

Chattahoochee-Oconee National Forests History
Brasstown District Ranger's Office
1881 Highway 515
P.O. Box 9
Blairsville, GA 30514
(706) 745-6928
Web site: http://www.fs.fed.us/conf/welcome.htm

Department of Historic Preservation and Heritage Tourism
City of Saint Augustine
P.O. Box 210
Saint Augustine, FL 32085-0201
(904) 825-5033
e-mail: cosa@ci.st-augustine.fl.us
Web site: http://www.ci.st-augustine.fl.us

DeSoto National Forest
654 West Frontage Road
P.O. Box 248
Wiggins, MS 39577
(601) 928-5291
Web site: http://www.fs.fed.us/r8/miss/

De Soto National Memorial
P.O. Box 15390
Bradenton, FL 34280-5390
(941) 792-0458
Web site: http://www.nps.gov/deso

Fort De Soto Park
3500 Pinellas Bayway South
Tierra Verde, FL 33715-2528
(727) 582-2267
e-mail: office@fortdesoto.com
Web site: http://fortdesoto.com

Hernando De Soto Historical Society
910 3rd Avenue West
Bradenton, FL 34205
(941) 747-1998
e-mail: desotohq@verizon.net
Web site: http://www.desotohq.com

Hernando de Soto State Archaeological Site
1022 De Soto Park Drive
Tallahassee, FL 32301
(850) 922-6007
Web site: http://www.vashti.net/taltrust/de_soto.htm

Parkin Archeological State Park
P.O. Box 1110
Parkin, AR 72373-1110
(870) 755-2500
e-mail: parkin@arkansas.com
Web site: http://www.uark.edu/campus-resources/
　　archinfo/parkin.html

Due to the changing nature of Internet links, the Rosen Publishing Group, Inc., has developed an online list of Web sites related to the subject of this book. This site is updated regularly. Please use this link to access the list:

http://www.rosenlinks.com/lee/heso/

# FOR FURTHER READING

Albornoz, Miguel. *Hernando de Soto—Knight of the Americas*. New York: Franklin Watts, 1986

Brown, Virginia Pounds. *Cochula's Journey*. Montgomery, AL: Black Belt Press, 1996.

Chrisman, Abbott. *Hernando de Soto*. Austin, TX: Raintree Steck-Vaughn, 1994.

Clayton, Lawrence A., et al. *The de Soto Chronicles: The Expedition of Hernando de Soto to North America in 1539–1543*. Tuscaloosa, AL: The University of Alabama Press, 1993.

Duncan, David Ewing. *Hernando de Soto: A Savage Quest in the Americas*. Norman, OK: University of Oklahoma Press, 1997.

Ewen, Charles R., and John H. Hann. *Hernando de Soto Among the Apalachee: The Archaeology of the First Winter Encampment*. Gainesville, FL: University Press of Florida, 1998.

Gallagher, Jim. *Hernando de Soto and the Exploration of Florida*. Broomall, PA: Chelsea House, 1999.

Galloway, Patricia Kay, ed. *The Hernando de Soto Expedition: History, Historiography, and Discovery in the Southeast*. Lincoln, NE: University of Nebraska Press, 1997.

Hudson, Charles. *Knights of Spain, Warriors of the Sun: Hernando de Soto and the South's Ancient Chiefdoms*. Athens, GA: University of Georgia Press, 1998.

Manning, Ruth. *Hernando de Soto*. Chicago: Heinemann, 2000.

Milanich, Jerald T., and Charles Hudson. *Hernando de Soto and the Indians of Florida*. Gainesville, FL: University Press of Florida, 1993.

Young, Gloria A., and Michael P. Hoffman, eds. *The Expedition of Hernando de Soto West of the Mississippi, 1541–154: Proceedings of the de Soto Symposia, 1988 and 1990*. Fayetteville, AK: University of Arkansas Press, 1999.

# BIBLIOGRAPHY

Clayton, Lawrence A., et al. *The de Soto Chronicles: The Expedition of Hernando de Soto to North America in 1539–1543*. Tuscaloosa, AL: The University of Alabama Press, 1993.

Duncan, David Ewing. *Hernando de Soto: A Savage Quest in the Americas*. Norman, OK: University of Oklahoma Press, 1997.

Ewen, Charles R., and John H. Hann. *Hernando de Soto Among the Apalachee: The Archaeology of the First Winter Encampment*. Gainesville, FL: University Press of Florida, 1998.

Galloway, Patricia Kay, ed. *The Hernando de Soto Expedition: History, Historiography, and Discovery in the Southeast*. Lincoln, NE: University of Nebraska Press, 1997.

Hudson, Charles. *Knights of Spain, Warriors of the Sun: Hernando de Soto and the South's Ancient Chiefdoms*. Athens, GA: University of Georgia Press, 1998.

Milanich, Jerald T., and Charles Hudson. *Hernando de Soto and the Indians of Florida*. Gainesville, FL: University Press of Florida, 1993.

Young, Gloria A., and Michael P. Hoffman, eds. *The Expedition of Hernando de Soto West of the Mississippi, 1541–154: Proceedings of the de Soto Symposia, 1988 and 1990*. Fayetteville, AK: University of Arkansas Press, 1999.

# INDEX

## About the Author

Jan Goldberg is an experienced, credentialed educator, and the author of thirty nonfiction books and hundreds of articles, textbooks, and other projects.

## Photo Credits

## Series Design

Tahara Hasan

## Layout

Les Kanturek

## Editor

Christine Poolos